ALL MORNING THE CROWS

Also by Meg Kearney

POETRY
An Unkindness of Ravens
Home By Now
The Ice Storm

VERSE NOVELS FOR TEENS:
The Secret of Me
The Girl in the Mirror
When You Never Said Goodbye

PICTURE BOOK:
Trouper

ALL MORNING
THE CROWS

Meg Kearney

WINNER OF THE 2020 WASHINGTON PRIZE
Andrea Carter Brown, Series Editor

THE WORD WORKS
WASHINGTON, D.C.

Inquire of:
The Word Works   P.O. Box 42164
Washington, D.C. 20015 / editor@wordworksbooks.org
Author photograph: Gabriel Parker
Cover design: Susan Pearce Design
Cover art: Craig Kosak

LCCN: 2021933065
ISBN: 978-1-944585-44-0

Acknowledgments

A heartfelt thank you to the editors of the following journals and anthologies for publishing these poems, some in earlier versions:

Agni Online: "Parrot" and "Partridge"
American Journal of Poetry: "Crow"
The Baltimore Review: "Starlings"
Beer, Wine, & Sprits Anthology, World Enough Press (James Bertolino, ed.): "Juncos" and "Petrels"
Bellevue Literary Review: "Oriole"
BigCityLit: "Bluebird"
Cave Wall: "Goldfinch" and "Geese"
Glimpse: "Chickadee," "House Finch," and "Mourning Doves"
Great River Review: "Bittern," "Ostrich," "Wren," and "Thrush"
Green Mountains Review: "Heron"
The Kenyon Review: "Scarlet Tanager"
Like Light: 25 Years of Poetry & Prose by Bright Hill Poets & Writers (Bertha Rogers, ed.): "Cuckoo" and "Eagles"
Massachusetts Review & The Best American Poetry 2017 (Natasha Trethewey, ed.): "Grackle"
Mead: "Albatross"
New Ohio Review: "Ibis"
Poetry East: "Owl" and "Woodpecker"
Post Road: "Penguins"
Prairie Schooner: "Pheasant"
Stone Canoe: "Barn Swallows" and "Warbler"
Missouri Review: "Loon"
Tar River Poetry: "Cormorant"
The Southampton Review: "Swallow"

"Loon" and "Warbler" were also part of the 2016 "Finding Place on Paper: Contemporary Poets and Printmakers Explore the White Mountains" exhibit at the Museum of the White Mountains (Plymouth State University). Thanks to Museum curators Liz Ahl, Parker Potter, and Cynthia Robinson for their support.

"Skimmer" is for Meg Dunn. "Juncos" is for Kevin McLellan. "Ibis" is for Cindy Zelman.

Many people have supported me during the writing of these poems, and in all of my literary endeavors: my beloved husband Gabriel Parker (my number-one supporter and cheerleader); Howard Levy (first reader and often second and third one, too); Steve Huff (second to read this manuscript through and offer invaluable help and encouragement); Tanya Whiton (who understood the story this book tries to tell, and suggested most of the poems' order); Laure-Anne Bosselaar; Meg Dunn de Pulido; Cornelius Eady; Lita Judge; Deborah Smith Bernstein; Jett and Shelley Whitehead; Fran Graffeo & Carol Hohman; Kathi Aguero; Kyle Potvin; Rick Bursky; Laura Williams McCaffrey; Mark Turcotte; Ian Haley Pollock; Sandra Scofield; Anne-Marie Oomen; Sarah Dunlap; Martha Rhodes; Barbara Unger; Donna Reis; Dave Cappella; Michael Waters; Cleopatra Mathis; Kwame Dawes; Renée Watson; Jacqueline Woodson; the late Donald Hall and the late Randall Kenan. Mariève Rugo was the generous friend who sent me Diane Ackerman's *The Genius of Birds*. Thanks, too, to Beth Little, Quintin Collins, and my entire community at the Solstice MFA in Creative Writing Program of Pine Manor College/Boston College.

A huge hunk of appreciation also goes to Koke Fedorowicz, Nancy Ferrara, and the Ferrara family for "adopting me" and letting me use their cabin in the White Mountains of New Hampshire every August for the last 30+ years; that's where the majority of these poems were drafted. Thanks also go to all of my friends connected with the Frost Place in Franconia, New Hampshire, where I grew up as a poet.

Deep gratitude is also due to everyone at The Word Works, including the committee members and editor Andrea Carter Brown for choosing this manuscript for the Washington Prize (thank you, too, for your poet's sharp eye, teamwork, and patience, Andrea!), and publisher Nancy White. I'm also grateful to Susan Pearce for her stunning cover design, and Craig Kosak for his marvelous painting.

My family has my gratitude and love always. In that spirit, I must thank my dog Trouper, who was my first listener and my companion throughout the writing of these and so many other poems. I miss his steady gaze, his one raised ear, his patient presence.

Contents

THREE

FOUR

For Gabriel

Bird, n:

1. a.I.1.a orig. The general name for the young of the feathered tribes;
a young bird; a chicken, eaglet, etc.; a nestling.
...d.I.1.d A maiden, a girl. ...In mod. (revived) use: a girl, woman
(often used familiarly or disparagingly) (slang).

—O.E.D.

Preface

My fascination with birds began in childhood as I stood at the dining room window next to my mother, watching blue jays chase off the chickadees, cardinals, and juncos vying for time at the feeder in our back yard. Often she kept her 1947 paperback edition of Peterson's *A Field Guide to Birds* within reaching distance. She'd shake her head in frustration at the jays, and sometimes rap her knuckles on the glass in an attempt to spook them. "Those greedy blue jays!" she'd exclaim as I nodded and joined in the knocking. She especially adored cardinals, and I wanted them to come back just to please her.

Members of the birding community should know that I am technically not a "birder." Throughout my life I have observed birds, and I have learned a few things about them along the way, but there are many back home in New York and right here in New England where I now live that I would fail to identify. I certainly do not know many by their songs. Simply, I am a bird lover who has written a book of poems inspired by—though technically not about—birds.

Listening to NPR in 2002, I heard a review of *100 Birds and How They Got Their Names* by Diana Wells (Algonquin Books of Chapel Hill, 2002). Thinking it could be a resource for poems, I ordered a copy. Years later, I acted on my idea, using each of Wells's descriptions as a prompt to write one hundred poems over the course of twelve months. In some, I relied on Wells's entertaining descriptions, while for others her brief essays simply provided a launching point.

I set the manuscript aside for three years, then picked up where I left off—jotting down observations, consulting Peterson's *Guide*, reading other texts and looking up details on the internet, re-writing—until it felt as if this "project" of mine had undergone some sort of magical transformation in order to tell a story. Please enjoy the endnotes that credit diction and ideas from *100 Birds* and other sources. I am deeply grateful to Diana Wells and the extraordinary histories and facts she shares, and hope this collection serves as a thank you.

—Meg Kearney
New Hampshire, October 2020

ONE

࣠

Owl

She birthed you, but she is so
    unknowable.
Is that the word? Try,
    nocturnal. Each night
she glides on wings silent
    as a vole quivering
under snow. Perched on your
    bedroom sill she watches
you dream-twitch, then spins
    her head to spy the snow-
mound ripple—sugary in moonlight—
    as the vole tunnels past pines.
She lifts off, silent still, and you—
    daughter of hurt and squeal—
are awake. When you sigh,
    your heart-shaped face
aches. Is that the word? Try,
    breaks, knowing when she dies
you'll inherit all she's swallowed
    whole yet had to leave behind.

Ibis

Her first mistake was trusting a god
with the body of a man and the head
of an ibis. People said he was old
and bald and croaked like a raven,
desired only shrimp and flies. But no.
No, he was fine and smelled of salt.
He knew her names, the one she was
born with and the one she was given.
Knowledge, he said, *is a pond awake*
with fish. When he stripped her
on its mossy bank and lured her in,
she understood. Lily pads tangled
around their knees. Her body was a map
his hands had drawn. Beyond clear blue
sky she saw the moon, full, and stars
in their constellations. If only she'd been
satisfied. Instead she tugged at his arm,
insisting. For wisdom he had to carry
her to shore, lay her down. She imagined
the earth would open, reveal its golden
center. But his bill was sharp. She thought
he would be gentle. Yet with each peck
he drove her deeper, deeper, until she knew
he had never truly been a wading bird
or bastard child—he was god of a heaven
where all the angels' bodies were broken.

Loon

I bought a cassette tape of loon calls so I could speak
their language that summer I camped on Russet Pond.
This was the eighties so cassette tapes were *the thing*—

side A was for *where-are-you-I-am-here* or *I-am-hungry*
calls, meaning hoots, wails, and peeps; side B was for
aggression and distress—yodels and tremolos, the latter

a kind of alarm laugh that led to the saying "crazy
as a loon." Kids today don't have the chance to choose
between side A and B—*B*, the poor man's intermission

or a sleeper song's second chance—but now I'm talking
45 records, 1972, with "Deeper and Deeper" on the B side
of "Billy Don't Be a Hero," which was more a tremolo

than a yodel, a sentimental, romantic, anti-war song
that slew my heart in third grade. No one I knew liked
"Deeper and Deeper," though on Russet Pond I learned

that loons, with their solid bones, can dive deeper and longer
than most birds; and I found I preferred wails to tremolos,
wails being the kind of call I'd perfected myself by then.

Crow

It was a crow first taught me
how to pry a thing open—snatch
a stick to leverage a headstone or widen
the hole in a rotten pine's trunk
to get at the story inside.

ﱡ

New York, 1999:

If our mother had kept you,
my newly found sister said,
you'd never have gone
to college. Wouldn't have done
a lot of things you've done.

ﱡ

Ornithologists claim crows have an innate sense
of fairness. One will scoff
at your proffered raisin, for example,
if you've given her sister two peanuts.

(If you've given her sister
away—that's a fact best kept cached
like the crows' scraps of roadkill
and white-oak acorns.)

ﱡ

I wasn't the first apprentice
to the crow, first to learn that old term
"crowbar." Handy for getting at grubs
and slugs or warding off a man
with a brick for a fist. Flip the bar
around to hook a beetle. But not
a mother. Not
a sister.

๑

—if she had kept me?

๑

A rooster crows;
crows caw. Explain that,
and while you're at it, how
you came to laugh my mother's
laugh, my newly found sister said.
I said, I never claimed to be anyone's
interpreter. She said, Our, I meant to say
our mother.

๑

Rhode Island, 1960:

Hear that? Crows are songbirds, too,
squawk the nuns in their choir loft.
See the one with a little silver cross
in her beak, jimmying the blue-gold window's
latch? That's her. My first mother.

๑

Our mother told me,
my newly found sister said,
she went to Catholic boarding school.
I said, Well—the convent...

Our mother did not speak
a secret language. She spoke
the language of secrets.

๑

As any ex-nun would tell you: the world
isn't simply black and white. Consider

a plum in a crow's beak in sunlight.
Consider the nun's habit, sunk
to its knees in the confessional's
dark. Color of a broken vow,
iridescent as a cancer cell.

つ

Apprentice, yes, I told
my newly found sister.
Ravens?
You have to work your way up
to ravens.

つ

Corpses. Cemeteries. What many people think
when they hear "crow," also known as
the pall-bearer of souls.

By the time I found her, my first mother
had already been dead
seventeen years. Why was I
surprised? At her grave
I left a silver earring
for the crows to find.

つ

Does anyone ever see a scarecrow and think
"crow"? Corn fields,
maybe. Or,
Father, is that you?

つ

If you leave us, the nuns in Bristol
told my first mother,
you will die a terrible death.
But she stole a dress blue
as a baby crow's eye
plus five hundred nickels.

Bought a bus ticket to Boston.
The dress? A newly arrived novitiate's.
"Crow's eye blue"? Code
for so sexy it was in
the to-be-burned bin.

ɔ

How did she go from Boston to New
York to Tucson? Why didn't she tell us
about you? my newly found sister wants
to know. She now thinks
I have the knowledge of crows.

ɔ

From the crow's nest of her get-away ship
my first mother could have seen
nothing useful. Not the snake-charmer with his
charming snake or Prince Charming or how
a daughter can shrink to a name on a dotted line,
to one wide brown eye on the horizon
before falling off the edge
of her world.

ɔ

In Scotland, crows are "corbies."
Grand-Dad never lost his brogue,
my newly found sister said.
She said she could still hear him singing
about the "twa corbies" who feast
on a dead knight's bonny-blue eyes.

ɔ

When still in her Sister Gabriella disguise,
my first mother taught second grade.
All those children, not one of them hers.
Snack-time milk box cost five cents.
Add it up.

Fact: crows can recognize human faces,
even remember them years later.

The first time I saw my mother in a photograph,
I thought it was some sort of trick
mirror. Hello, I said. I know you.

You are she
when I last remember her well,
my newly found sister said.

No place for a ship in Arizona, meaning
no daily departures leaving from Boston
or New York, where I was harbored. Was that
the allure? To be far from the Atlantic,
its relentless chant. Though the desert
is its own type of sea.

She was given a photograph of me to keep.
Grief came in waves like the heat.

On overcast days—before clocks—
Jews began the Sabbath
when crows came home to roost.
Crows don't need a timepiece—
sunset's when all the good stuff
starts to happen.

ɔ

Arizona, 1983:

(This the story I've been told, with a few guesses thrown in.)

Round and around my first mother's deathbed
flew the Sisters of Bristol, that murder
of crows.
I have another daughter, she whispered
to her husband. Low, so her children
wouldn't hear.
He promised to find me. Thinking
this would make her live.

ɔ

Told you so, chanted the crows
settling like a wreath at her feet.

ɔ

How did she get to Tucson?
Some say the southern route, a brand-new
Corvair convertible.
I say she flew.

Warbler

By early winter the warbler
is gone, but its song lingers
the way a hike up Cannon
Mountain lingers in the knees,
or the smell of smoke

hovers in the cabin
on foggy mornings, embers
cool and damp, even,
like the newspaper and her
books. She should have

headed south by now,
too.
      Soon. When she runs
out of wood. Scrounging
for kindling at the forest's

edge, sitting wrapped
in a blanket where sun
hits the porch—she hears
that bird at the oddest
times: *please please*

pleased to MEET-cha—
this afternoon as she's
headed to the spring
with her jug. The dog
doesn't seem to notice,

for here is the path
blazed by deer to where
they drink. Maybe the dog's
company isn't enough.
She's hearing things.

Or, like her, one bird
has stayed past all
warnings. There it is
again. From the porch
she can't see the mountains—

it's snowing in the Notch.
We should go now,
she tells the dog.
Black as the top of Cannon
is white, he settles

on the hearth rug.
She crisscrosses
sticks over crumpled
paper, finds matches
in the little blue cupboard.

Goldfinch

Goldfinch tore at the crown of thorns on the crucified
Christ's brow, but only flew away with bloodied cheeks
and a mournful song. It pricked like a thistle, shoved all
other music from his breast. His one-song repertoire
he now called Elegy, Calvary, Skull Place, or Mother
Do Not Weep, depending on the season, the pallor
of the sky, how empty his belly and how hungry the lion
pawing the amphitheater ground. Goldfinch couldn't
snatch that crown, much less save a quaking flock
from martyrdom. How the crowd roared when the lion
pulled that first man down! Wailing for Jesus, women
sank to their knees. Men scattered like seeds. Goldfinch
watched the rows of virgins in their flawless ribbons rise,
better to see the girl they knew as Hannah, now a blue rag
in the lion's mouth. The bird sang O Sacred Body, he sang
Lord Have Mercy and Do Not Forsake Me while the sated
lion yawned, his ruby tongue blooming in the sun.

Duckling, Swan

Before I was born I was biggest of the clutch, already a burden
and slow to hatch. When at last I smashed my way into this world,
my mother's tongue unfurled a hiss, siblings snickered and jeered.
Who could love an ugly girl, smothered in egg wax, gray as the curl
in a drowned man's lip? Even cleaned up, my down was ash. I was the art
of my mother's mistake, the ache in her dinosaur heart. I was the winter,
the ice-over early, no fish in the pond and the hunter's sure shot. I had
nowhere to go when they drove me out; I went like something dead
in coyote's mouth. Like something a cat mauled then tossed about.
I starved through the full moons. Slept in the snow. But by spring a lake
was aglow with my gleaming—in spring I returned and blinded them all.

Penguins

They looked like little children
standing upright on the shore
the sailors said, still at sea.
All were hungry under that frozen sun.

Standing upright on the shore,
a cluster of fathers and their chicks—
all were hungry under that frozen sun
waiting for the mother penguins' return.

The cluster of fathers and their chicks
didn't see the sailors land—
waiting for the mother penguins' return
they'd survived brutal nights, furious blizzards.

They didn't see the sailors land
(axes, knives, and clubs in hand);
they'd survived brutal nights, furious blizzards,
the stunning tails of killer whales.

Axes, knives, and clubs in hand
the sailors made quick work of slaughter.
The stunning tails of killer whales,
wolves' teeth—nothing had ever slain so many.

The sailors made quick work of slaughter.
How many dead penguins could a ship hold?
Wolves, whales—nothing had ever slain so many.
What haunts sailors' dreams: penguins, huddled on shore.

How many dead penguins a ship can hold!
the sailors said, back at sea.
What haunts sailors' dreams: huddled on shore,
penguins look like little children.

House Finch
Long Island, New York, 1940

Most arrived in wood and wire cages;
some, in brass domes—all to be sold
as pets to lovers under umbrellas packed
spoke-to-spoke on Jones Beach, or

to the Smiths of Smithtown enjoying
their backyard beer and barbeque
afternoons. Soon, the house finch,
let loose, would populate the east

just as the Smiths and Joneses were
doing, copulating like good Catholics
until even the gulls couldn't
compete. But that summer, 1940,

"Hollywood Finches" were as exotic
as Mai Tais, another splash of
California color newly arrived
to the North Shore. There, the Smiths

still preferred their Budweiser and Irish
whiskey, but they did applaud the release
of the finches. My first mother was
a young girl then, maybe thirty inches

tall, barely big enough to fetch Papa
Smith a beer. She had nothing to fear,
warbling around the yard like a bird.
She didn't yet know how a cage

can spring up around you, spirit you
away, and alone. She didn't yet know
that once the door clicks shut behind
you, there's no going home.

Starlings

All the starlings I have known are dead.
Summers I'd scrape them off the school
house lawn—their nests on the edge
of a slate blue roof—babies featherless,
heads too heavy, breathing shallow
as promises of drunks. I've known a few
of *them*, too, heads dipping and rising
before the final plunk. There's only so
much you can do, which by age seven
or eight I knew about drunks, but baby
birds I thought might be saved with
an eye-dropper filled with milk. Some
mushed up worms. What I wanted
to shove down their throats was song,
echo of their parents' cartoon chirps,
their imitation coughs of crows that
peppered the school yard willow.
Damn. Starlings will mimic anything:
drunkard's bellow, eighteenth-century
allegretto. Mozart once bought a pet
starling when it whistled his G major
concerto. He was flattered, I am sure,
though maybe too like me he thought
a song could save a thing. Could save
a starling, anyhow. I buried those
babies on the school's vast grounds.
Marked the place with stones. Winters
I would visit there while my mother
drank alone. *Quiet*, I'd tell the babies'
ghosts as their murmuration rose
far above the school house roof
its belly full of stars.

Cardinal
1960

Maybe all along it wasn't God, but a bird
who had called her years before. What else
explains this urge for flight from these
convent walls? She refuses to heed her own
heart's ominous hisses. She might confuse

the devil with a high priest with the bird
she heard during vespers—red fused in her
mind along with that cursed girl in the fairy-
tale who pricks her finger on a spindle. Briar
Rose was only doomed until the Prince—

is it he her heart truly fears? She has no time
for princes, or a hundred years. Once she read
a caged cardinal sings, then dies of grief.
She must steal herself away—or so a cardinal's
trill convinces: *Remember, Jesus loved a thief.*

TWO

Heron

We scared the shit out of her, that heron—
not what the dog and I expected in a thicket
of pine half a mile from Cranberry Meadow
Bog. The bird hoisted herself into the air, left
a streak of white like a run of watery paint
across the rock she'd rested on. She crashed
her way through the forest, wide wings
cracking boughs that tore at her feathers
as she fled.
      Fear can make any girl oblivious
to branches shredding her arms and legs
as she makes her escape—say, from a man
running after her with a brick. That's so far
in the past, but *she* was the one who believed
love could change a drunk—until she saw
what he held in his hand.
      Enough. Now I simply pity that girl
and the heron, who couldn't know
we meant her no harm.

Bittern

I thought nothing of walking alone
on the trail along the river until
the photographs in the paper,

whispers at the hardware store
and post office. The men had
dragged them both but tied only

the mother, stuffed her own socks
in her mouth. It must have taken
hours, what they did then, until

they were through. A hiker found
the body first, blood where they'd
cut off her clothes and got sloppy.

A few yards away the girl sat
among the cattails and tall grasses.
The birds were silent but not

the crickets. She tilted her head—
all crimson patches—stared directly
at the sun. In her lap, that nest

of auburn hair. Her slender body
swayed slightly in the autumn
breeze, like all the other reeds.

Flicker

Birth Mother on the Run

She's been hoping for a sign. Seeking one.
So the silver glint glimpsed from the corner
of her eye—as if God had flipped a coin
and it flickered as it fell, nickel of sun
spent quick as breath—seems more
than just a bird. She can't quite tell

where she is. An hour, maybe, into
Tennessee. She could stop to eat—sirloin,
a Coke to stay awake. Figure out what the hell
such a sign might mean.

There's no going back.
It can't mean that but she keeps driving just to
be sure. Maybe the flicker signifies what it cost
to leave. Her baby, asleep in that room. Crack
of light before the door shut and all was lost.

Grackle

What a grackle is doing perched on the rail
of her baby's crib, noiselessly twitching its
tail, she doesn't wonder. The way this baby
gleams he's bound to catch a grackle's
eye. Besides, birds have flit in and out
of these baby dreams forever. Sapsucker,
blue jay. Sparrow, kingfisher, titmouse.
She just likes to *say* grackle, a crack-your-
knuckles, hard-candy word. In the dream,
her baby's black as a grackle, meaning
when she holds him to the light he shines
purple and blue, a glittery bronze. Silent
and nameless. Sometimes he is a she but
always the dream-baby is hers. That is
the miracle. Nights of nursery rhymes
and sorrow. Of yellow quilts and song
birds. Enough to break a bough. Enough
to fell a cradle.

Petrels

Our ship in its bottle is forever
tossed at sea. Two petrels follow
lee side. Two in our wake. There's
ice in the rigging; life-boats all are
fake. Petrels seem to walk on water
but skim the surface for our chum.
Each night we spew that over-
board, rinse our stinking mouths
with rum. I knew it was a dumb idea
to climb aboard this ship. Said it just
before you offered that first nip.
Before the petrels. Before the squall.
Before the bottle made us small.

Albatross

Forget sailors. You never trusted them,
though the one who approached you
on the beach, spoke to you as if you were
a woman, you in the new bikini
none of the boys back home had noticed—
he and his friends could have put an end to all
that was good in you, over behind the boulders
at low tide. You sat with them in a circle
playing gin. They smelled of salt and sweat
and you were too flattered to flee, though
the constant surf said *Leave. Leave.* When you
finally said you were fifteen, they stared
at each other over their cards, and that was
the last game. They picked you up, sat you
down where they found you by the sea,
like a piece of glass that needed more time
in the waves before it could be called
beautiful. They were good sailors. You had
asked if they knew the poem, but when they
shook their heads no, you let the story
go, looked down at your hearts and spades.

Blue Jays
At the 7-Eleven

Since December's storm
the girl on morning shift
throws donuts to the jays.
Powdered sugar dusts their
ice-blue jackets; grape jelly
flecks their beaks. Weekdays
there for coffee, I linger
for their antics: two, three
flapping jays screeching
like bus brakes in the back
lot, girl waving a donut box
to clear out all the crumbs.
She's too young to know
this store was once a bar.
I swayed near this very spot
to sober up, take in a few
stars. Practiced in the art
of gin, I watched the new
drunks start their cars. Back
then I had an owl's heart.
All the jays were sleeping.

Skimmer

At the Country Club

Our boss John was like that bird,
skimmed the pool of our tips
without getting his belly wet.
His tongue was a blade
that cut if we dropped a cup

or couldn't lift a six-top's
dinner on a single tray. We girls
held each other up, helped each
other out, like POWs in a work
camp. Desperate for money, we

would have revolted if we'd known
he was feeding off us night- and
day-shift and especially during
weddings when the bride's father,
always more shell-shocked than

trashed, slipped John extra cash
"for the lovely staff." He skimmed
that the way his namesake skims
an estuary at high tide—fast
and efficient. We suspected

but could not catch him until one
summer evening Chef spied the top
of John's head flying not quite low
enough below the kitchen window;
in his arms, a case of *Veuve*

Clicquot. Chef tackled him while
Dora called the cops, who arrived
to find John's Lexus stocked
with the club bar's top shelf. We
always said he had good taste—

he'd hired us. We partied late
that night, toasted the sight of John
in cuffs and John's last glance at us,
his coked-up pupils wild, pissed,
slit like a skimmer's or a snake's.

Swifts

Mornings back in her attic apartment days—that ghost-gray house
shipwrecked between the railroad tracks and the river—swifts
streamed by her skylight like a ribbon, twisted, then lifted up
and east toward town. By dusk they were funneling above

the chimneys, six crumbling roosts the second-floor boys planned
to raid should they discover a recipe for swift soup, the boys
students at the Culinary Institute, drawn to menus of the unusual
and bizarre. "Flying cigars," they nicknamed those birds. Blunt

heads and squared-off tails color of dried tobacco. When she lit
a spliff, cranked ZZ Top, the boys pounded on her trapdoor to come
up. What did she know about lust? Not enough. The whole house
shook with it each time a train rumbled by. She'd pile her books

on the door, along with the ladder, its coil of rope. Two friends
had said *Buy a gun*, but she could never—. Swifts circled her
skylight twice before setting down. A sign, she'd hope, the door
would foil those soon-to-be chefs, baying by then like hounds.

Wren

It's a winter wren, mouselike
and secretive, that's made
a home in the pocket of my
old canvas coat. Hanging

on a nail inside the tool shed,
that coat's kept a couple
of generations dry—why
not another. Besides, the bird's

nest solves a mystery:
I'd thought I'd heard a song sparrow,
that hard, two-syllable *kimp kimp*
call, but I couldn't place

those high, tinkling warbles tucked
deep in the ferns and thick underbrush
beyond the weeping willow. Once
I thought I'd heard God calling

from there. That turned out to be
an uncommon bird, too—
at least it didn't appear in any
guide. One book says

it's not uncommon to find a house
wren nesting in your coat
pocket. A winter wren
is favored by mummers, those

straw boys of Dingle playing
penny whistles through their motley
masks, begging a tuppence to bury
the bird on St. Stephen's Day.

Why do the Irish martyr a wren
to honor St. Stephen? You'll have
to ask them. William Blake warned
against it, but they aren't about to

allow some Englishman mar a custom,
even if he was a great poet.
Which brings me back to this
wren in my pocket. Its name

might come from the Swedish
vrensk, "uncastrated," or the Anglo-
Saxon *wroene*, "lascivious."
Prostitutes were once called

"wrens," another reason why
I'll leave this nest alone, not
feeling righteous enough
to cast the first stone.

Partridge

For miles and miles lush hedgerows were alive
with our toe-scratch and egg heat; our chatter
louder than bees, making green leaves flutter.
We hatched into this world wide-eyed; arrived
covered in down. By the time the scythe
swept the fields we were chestnut-barred and fatter,
all belly patch and seed-hungry. Better
to remember our red-throated love calls than try
to forget that first blast of dog, panicked
kuta-kuta cries, wing shudder as we
rose into light, dust, thunder-crack and star
bursts.
          Some of us tumbled from the air like leaves.
The rest of us blinked in tall grass as dogs licked
then lifted them gently. Black noses beat like hearts.

Robins

You were gone what, four days, and already
they've rebuilt their cup of mud and grass
upon the ledge above the porch screen door.
It sheds its telltale twigs, wisps of hay across
the stone stoop; you know there will be hell
to pay if you let it go—all that swooping—
and more crap to sweep. Heading to the shed
for gloves and a crate to stand on, you regret
what you've already ruined—last week's nest,
a magnificent spider's web (you'd spin it back
if you could), your own chance at motherhood.
At least the robins will learn, move on before
it's too late to propagate a brood or two.
The crate creaks but doesn't break as you rise
on tip-toe, robins now high in the oak's
new green, screeching out their *No*'s.

Plovers
Old Orchard Beach, Maine, Summer 1985

Like these plovers, I'm just passing through.
Plovers newly arrived from Florida along
with the rest of the snow birds. Seventy-

five El Camino, huffing like an old dog,
is what got us here. The guys chugged beer
the entire drive. Okay, so did I. Check out

these plovers, slinging back sand flies.
Another one of those trips we were lucky
to survive. Guide book says in medieval

times a plover could tell whether a man
would live or die. Maybe some plover
looked me in the eye as I poured myself

onto this beach, more drunk than alive.
Deemed me too dumb to die. Yet. Up-
beach body builders oil their biceps while

the guys fetch Margaritas from the Tiki
bar. One's my lover, the other along for
the ride. Mark. Like the apostle. I'm not

really dumb, just five on a scale of one to—
guide says plover's name comes from
the Latin word for rain, but doesn't explain

why. Each time I say "bride," Mark's face
looks like rain. But who am I? Too good
for what? Now the guys, still at the bar,

wave frosted glasses—faces frosted, too.
No doubt they've sniffed a line. No booze,
they mime, allowed on the beach. Coked-

up love. A loaded vow. Might not get better
than that, I tell Mark. Tonight this crowd will
recede like the tide. Not the guys—too high,

I'm sure, to find our motel. I'll dig a seat here
in the sand. Watch the moon rise. Plovers
will sleep in the shallows where they hide.

Geese

*There are voices we hear in solitude, but they grow faint
and inaudible as we enter the world.*
—Ralph Waldo Emerson

February. What few geese had bothered
to head south were already back, a honking
skein threading through clouds above Concord
Prison like a woman sending her silk-scarf
signal to her confined lover. From his cell
window he watched them land in the nearby
cornfield to feast and shit their way to Walden
Pond. He'd had a new song in his head;
it started playing itself hours before to the tune
of twenty men snoring through a fluorescent
blare. He had his pad of paper; his pencil hovered
in the air as the first word grew fat and then
the geese pecked at the thread and blew:
Everybody's Got the Blues. But that's been sung
already, he said out loud, and the song—like his
woman and the gaggle beyond—stretched its wings
and flew.

Woodpecker

Leave home for a few weeks
and you might return to find
a yellow-bellied sapsucker
drilling your mountain ash,

forty-four holes in neat little
rows where the main branch
meets the trunk. It's not like
coming back to find your love

in bed with another. Both
of them still drunk. Of all
the things that have happened,
that's not one of them. It's

more like the shot glasses
you'd line up on the bar
when Mark Miller or Sam
What's His Name said he was

buying a round for a Friday-
night crowd. You'd mix up
a pitcher of pineapple peckers,
then fill all the glasses

in a single pour. You'd knock
one back, but stop at that—
peckers will sneak up on you,
everything real good until

it isn't. The tree was healthy
when you left. Now you've got
to hope that sapsucker had his
fill—things could take a bad

turn if he comes strutting
back, flashing that wing patch
and fancy red hat, thinking
he's a regular.

Cowbird

The brown hoodie should have been
her first clue. If not that, then his name—
Molobrus, which he claimed was Greek

for Lion-Hearted: steeped in courage,
fierce in the art of true love. It seemed
beneath her to look it up. It did cross

her mind to find that old textbook, but
by then he was on her stoop, baseball
glove waving atop a worn Eagle Scout

backpack (another fact that threw her
off). A suitcase in each hand. (How long—
had she said? Not a month, or a year?) Would

she hold the door? She couldn't speak.
There was more in the car—his shot-glass
collection, a box of LPs, that deer-antler

lamp and two amps for the band. He knew
she wouldn't mind—they'd be here soon,
too. They called themselves "Brood."

They were birds of a feather. What was
that he smelled? Roast beef, or stew?
Enough for five, he was sure. Which

way to their room? He'd tune up while
she cooked. He adored her guitar.
(A fine tradition to start: he'd play

as she worked.) She held his gaze,
asked for his rent. He sang "Love Me
Do" but that's not what she meant.

Magpie

They say I talk too much. *That Magpie, she's*
a chatterer, they say—Rather than ride
inside the ark with us, she perches
on the roof and croons away, just to please
herself while the whole world drowns. Horrified
I risk the storm to speak (rain merciless
for thirty days now, with no sign of stopping)
they act as if they've been sitting in church
while I've frolicked like the Devil's mistress.
Of course there are some who think women should
keep their beaks shut, just look pretty while mopping
everyone's shit off the floor. But tell me this:
if they all play it safe, simply wait for an end to the flood,
then who else will sing the song of witness?

Parrot

You are not a sudden
shadow, squeak and blood

on snow; not the rush
of wind and swoop, burst

of feathers in mid-air.
Whore's companion

and Adam's first bride,
parrot you are honey-

tongued lover
and the dog's wide

yawn; you're the mower's
green grumble

and the cowbird's song.
Oh you mushy-hearted

fruit-blue macaw, your
brilliant clown joy

is contagious. Give us your
butter-throated warble,

your coy bel canto
and ring-tone echo

while we madly pat
our pockets for our phones.

Eagles

From the power plant roof they can see north—Poughkeepsie,
lights on the bridge. When they face south they see even farther,
past Newburgh-Beacon's bridge to the prow of a barge being tugged
upriver. Its belly full of oil the next shift will unload. She stands
apart from the men. She's just the tour guide, not part of them, though

they both seem kind and showed her the way here: a metal ladder
then the door that lifts like a lid. Eagles, they'd said. Nests nearby.
Mornings a show as the birds ride valley air, scanning the Hudson
for striped bass or shad or whatever is running. Maybe none are
hungry today. Unlike the insatiable machines below, boilers

a story high. The turbines' ceaseless spinning make a whole city go.
What she tells the school kids and Boy Scouts earning badges,
so every time they flip a switch they think Roseton, think Danskammer,
the plant next door named by the Dutch who sailed up the river, spotted
a whorl of Indians on that point of land, and called it The Devil's

Dance Chamber. Danskammer, spewing its blackish *plume*, officially
never "smoke." Ever. Max lights a spliff. Pablo shakes his head no, but
Max says, She won't mind. The smoke's sweet punk makes her quiver.
Max says he's seen an eagle dive then burst from the surface, eel a live
rope in its talons. Pablo takes a toke. Offers the joint. He remembers

she's done this before. Wasn't she here with the coal-burning boys?
Quite a party, they'd heard. Her face, streaked with soot. She stops mid-
drag. Already the pot's ruffling the edges of her brain. She takes a full hit
before handing it back. *The kids who come here think the eagles are bald,*
she says—*It's just that their head feathers are white.* Max waves the joint.

She's as smart as they say. Her head's all a whirl but she's ready to run.
She's lean and lank and faster than they. The door's right behind her. Shut
but not locked. Her brain a flag unfurled. Heart, all flutter and angst.
Max flicks the roach, turns to the river and points. At eye level three
eagles circle then soar as if racing the train on the opposite bank.

Kingfisher

On calm days she wears a dress to work.
Tries to look normal. Pretty, even. Pretends
it's always like this, tranquil as the air
outside the office building and the just-
visible sea. Air conditioning an excuse
to wear her white cardigan so no one notices
her arms. The cuts bandaged but not healing.
At first she had used her fingernails. Now
prefers the knife. Just enough pain to distract
from his absence or the drinking or the long
stretches when a roar fills the house. When
the floorboards roil and churn and she feels
she might drown. He is there then with four
or five others. Stainless-steel pot on the stove.
Mirror, razor blade on the table. Glass bong
someone bought in Vietnam. After they smoke
the roar rises, a wave above her head. Fills her
mouth and ears. She lies down against the rocking,
their bedroom sometimes a harbor. There
her arms are a kind of chore, like scrubbing
the hull of a boat. By the time he remembers
her she is asleep. Or bluffing. He brings
weather with him—a gust or a gale. Acrid,
salt-choked. That past-tired greed. She thinks
of the girl Halcyone transformed into a bird,
how the god of wind calmed the sea all
around her. Just for a few days she'd floated
without fear. How the girl hadn't known this
would happen when she threw herself in.

Limpkin

Eliza Summer was hanging socks on the backyard line
when she heard it. Clothespins rained on the ground.

Lord have mercy, she prayed. Her hound lifted his
head to howl, then changed his mind. Diane Johnson

and her son Kip were peeling potatoes when they heard it.
Out on their porch, Kip still held his knife. Diane touched

his arm as if to ask, *Hear that?* Kip claimed it was a bird,
but Eliza knew it was that newlywed girl in the old white

house. Mary. It was a limpkin, Kip insisted, the swamp—.
His mother clucked. What did a boy know about heartbreak?

When Jen Kroll heard it, she called her father for the first time
in thirteen years. Joe Sprague slipped in the tub when he heard

it, and Paul Hoag at the diner shook coffee in his eggs. Diane
whispered, *That Mary came in the clinic last week, forearms*

shredded like—. She took Kip's knife. Nudged him. *Go shoot*
baskets. Sissy Freer cut off the tip of one braid with a tree pruner

when she heard it. Diane wished she didn't know about Mary.
Inside the house, she crossed herself, lit the wrong end

of a cigarette. When she called him in, Kip missed his shot.
He knew plenty about heartbreak. He'd had a father.

Nuthatch

He's too busy hacking acorns to sing
much. His name, after all, comes from
Old English, *hakken*, meaning "to
break" or "to cleave." Leave a chestnut
wedged between those white pickets
you've been painting this fall, then wait
for the crack of his blow. He can dish out
a good pounding better than your ex. Yes,
you know that sound too well, don't you.
If you're thinking what I'm thinking, stop.

All you know about fists will serve you
next time there's one or two to dodge.
The nuthatch, meanwhile, could teach
about scaling trees and keeping randy
rats from crawling through your door.
(All it takes is a blister beetle, a bit of
mud.) And sure, per above, he's an expert
nut buster. *That* could come in handy.

Barn Swallows

Bird shit will strip paint off a truck
as sure as your ex cleaned you out
of near everything you owned. So

as swallows circle and swoop 'round
rafters overhead, their colony of nests
sweating mud in the half-dark, you

spread a tarp over the cab. *Coked up
birds*, you think; then, *Cops covered
his body, his face like this*. More birds

sweep out the barn door and soon are
back, feasting on flies that still haunt
the empty horse stalls. Before you

cover the cap you peer through its glass—
they're there: rolled-up mat, sleeping bag
that formed your bed after how many

midnight escapes. *Don't count*. Once
he stole those, too, along with your
shoes, but after a seventy-hour high

he passed out and you stole them back
then disappeared for days. That was
an art you shared, but he finally

perfected. When they buried him
it rained so hard the ground seemed to
suck him under. It was mud tried to

steal your shoes then, while the preacher
told of Christ as a boy molding mud
into swallows that up and flew away.

THREE

Chickadee

White Mountains, New Hampshire

She's reached a new low in loneliness:
now she thinks the chickadee returns her call.

Dozy with noon heat and still wet from their walk
to the spring, the dog opens one eye as she steps

from the porch, blows a sort of *TOO-hoo* toward
three scrubby pines behind the cabin. In bare feet

she picks her way across the grass. Calls again.
Waits. All winter back home while the dog

napped she waited at the window with the cats,
watching chickadees spill a thimble-full of seed

from the feeder for each seed they snatched. That
silent show making the hollow space inside her

echo only louder with the footsteps of her dead.
Her father. Two mothers. Lately, too many

friends. When the chickadee goes silent she calls
H, who knows why each summer she comes

to this cabin alone with her dog. H lives in
the city. She may as well be in the nineteenth

century, up here in Franconia whistling
to birds. "Just like Wordsworth," she tells H—

"Remember? In *The Prelude*?" "Screw
Wordsworth," H says. The chickadee resumes

his namesake call: *chicka-dee-dee-dee*. She
loves H even when he's cruel. Still, a chill blows

through her hollows. H has to go. Listen: there's
the bird. She whistles back. So what. She's a fool.

And here is the dog, come again to fetch her.
He leans, damp fur of his hip cool against her

knee. The pines are silent as he turns and she
follows, back to the shade of the porch.

Juncos

I can't pour this bird seed from cup
to feeder without seeing my mother
pour a Scotch. I
can't.

After they cut out her lung
I said, "I'll call you every day."
She said, "Did you call
then hang up?"
"Don't bother," my brother said.
"She never remembers."

Now I'm standing on the back deck
of the house in New Hampshire,
a cup of bird seed in my hands.

Now I'm standing on the roof
of my old building on East 20th Street
watching the Towers fall.

Now I'm sneaking into my childhood
home in LaGrange, thinking
of juncos. Their gray-white bodies
like a building smoldering.

Bird seed turns golden, poured into
morning air.

Bird seed is not whiskey, but— .

"Bird seed—it's in your hair,"
my mother said, reaching for me.

Cuckoo

On a Golden Anniversary

Each time the viridian bird emerges through the front door
of the little house, the shutters fly open and all the couples

inside twirl in their dirndl dresses, lederhosen, and alpine
feathered hats first this way, then that. In her melodious

kitchen the widow still agrees each hour is a thing to celebrate.
But tonight, when the shutters close and the yellow-billed bird

back-pedals just before the red door clicks shut, she stands there,
brandishing that old crook-handled cane, demanding to be told

what the hell they're all doing in that house without her. Does
she smell a trace of cigar, hear a bottle being passed around?

It's not the first door slammed in her face. But it's the first one
she'll smash—

        though this chestnut stick was his. And the clock—
well, the clock, like her heart, is winding down.

Ostrich

Politicians, wishing to criticize eruditely . . . could safely
call rivals 'struthonian,' meaning that, like foolish ostriches, they
refuse to acknowledge reality.
　　　　　　—Diana Wells, *100 Birds and How They Got Their Names*

It took her two years to face it: he wasn't a nightingale.
He wasn't a mockingbird, either. Shit, he couldn't even
sing. When he promised her music, he'd meant
the store-bought kind, the brand that comes in a can.
And yet he didn't understand why she packed her
things, dressed for departure. You—you're depressed,
he said. She said No, she just had to save herself,
couldn't wait for a cavalry rescue. But they're nearly
here, he replied, laying his head on the ground, right
ear down. As he listened for the sound of hooves
she knew he was truly *struthonian*, and wanted to cry.
This bird not only couldn't sing, he couldn't fly.

Meadowlark

What the meadowlarks were doing back in Wyoming
while he diddled in the Blue Ridge she considered
much later. At that mountain retreat, the air was sweet
with briars and time unfurling and so their cast lines
tangled. Thoughts of meadowlarks, those superhero-
yellow breasts marked by triangles of black, came only
after he didn't head back west but followed her home

to New York. After the lone winters, the roses dried
in a bowl, roses color of red wine once it's turned.
Popcorn blossomed then burned on the stove as he said
I'm your man now, quit your job, I've got dinner
covered. She could feel one eyebrow rise like a flag.
He in his mind still living in Thailand, 1981, where
the Hmong thought him a savior. He could have been,

she first supposed—it was a romantic thought like his
meadowlarks' fluty morning melodies hovering above
the prairie or like the roses, which never did open.
He was a Rhodes Scholar in denim, a dentist's son, a cow-
boy complete with guitar, waistline beginning to thicken.
And surely, once his father died, he was too damn
grief-stricken to work, seeing as she still had hers.

He and his guitar might as well head to the bar, where
somebody's bound to know "My Horses Ain't Hungry"
while west in Wyoming meadowlarks nest in the hoof-
prints of stallions. That's a real fact, a detail the city
crowd eats up. Details, like Frisbees in Central Park,
a fast way to make friends. It was details that lured him
downtown that day the Towers fell. He left her with

a dead phone line; cell useless, too, but she had time then
for her penny whistle and of course the view. Not having
a horse he rode his bike as far as MacDougal or maybe
Jay Street. The day still sickly sunny above the cloud
of humans hovering there. New ghosts don't care for
voyeurs lured by tragedy. Buoyant as meadowlarks
they glided in low, made sure he breathed in a lung-full.

That's what she imagined from her twelfth-story perch.
That's when his stories lost their gleam. Later she heard him
describe that day as if it happened just to him.
By then she knew things aren't always what they seem:
a meadowlark isn't a lark at all, but cousin to the black-
bird—a detail he'd delete from his tales of cowboy
glory, as he was loath to let a fact ruin a good story.

Catbird

This morning low in the quince bush
catbird calls *Please. Please.* Summary
of what she's said to God for the last
thirty years. Her quiet quirts and catty

mews. Black-hooded words with somber-
gray bodies. A dried-blood red hidden
beneath their tails. When she isn't
begging she still keeps to the bushes thick

with quince, apple-like but bitter. *Try it,*
she coos, with desire enough to rival a dozen
Eves. Pretending then God can't hear.
Her song the catbird's repertoire, top-forty

picks of lust and seduction borrowed from
a backyard jukebox. But God knows
it's a ruse. Her heart's gone mealy and dry—
not enough sugar to make a quince pie.

Flamingo
South of Arles, France

She flees to the Camargue
where shrimp turn flamingos
a deep-pink hue. Locals claim

mosquitoes, those phony birds,
balloon big and mean enough
to carry them all away. That is

her desire—escape—but
the thousand flames lighting up
the marsh on yellow match-stick

legs seem so *American.* "I have
flown to France to land in Disney,"
she complains, and there rides

a cowboy in spurs just to prove it.
She's had enough of cowboys,
real and wannabes, or anything

that turns its head upside-down
to eat. What she needs lies
in the nearby village, St. Marys-

by-the-Sea, where rumors of
a miracle and a famed Gypsy
liquor bring her to her knees.

Oriole

To build their nest they stole my mother's cigarettes.
Next they snagged her booze. They took her heating
pads and measuring cups. Plucked her blood-soaked
tissues, bright as carnations, from the waste basket;
they took her shopping list, zip-up boots, Katrina
the cat, feeding tube. Her glasses and the book on her
lap. Filched her Sweet Dreams Tea, her *Field Guide
to Birds*. It wasn't all in this order, but they stole her
Easter wreath, the tumor in her throat, ironing board,
perfect penmanship, black-silk slip, her late night bowl
of ice cream and Cool Whip. They tried to take her last
words, but she snatched those back, took those with her.

Mourning Doves

New York, 2001

Mourning doves wake me, one pair resting
on my twelfth-story sill, billing and cooing.

Get up, said my mother in a dream. *There is
much left to weep over. Sleep is for the dead.*

She should know. Here, in the city, the dead
are the air we breathe. Bits of paper, they ride

the breeze; musical notes, they fly down
the mourning dove's throat, rise again

as dirge. Only music can mine such sorrow.
My mother never could carry a tune. Now

my doves go quiet as a hawk rides the thermals
between the ghosts of Tower One and Tower Two.

FOUR

Scarlet Tanager

1893

After too much New York City noise—
off-key and birdless—Dvořák rode out
to Iowa, that little Bohemia, to find
himself a little *scherzo*. He'd already
written his Requiem, married his true love's
sister. What he needed then was something
molto vivace, something quirky, full of off-
beats and cross-rhythms, something American.
Enter: the scarlet tanager. No matter Thoreau
disliked the bird's "harsh notes" and his
own wife said it sounded like a robin
with a sore throat—from an oak's green canopy
came the high, interrupting strain of a violin
on fire. Next came the second violin, a viola,
a cello, a gapped pentatonic composed by nature,
a scarlet-plumed opus, folk-like but stranger;
next came an American Quartet in F major.

Thrush

Deep in the forest behind my cabin, a wood
thrush plays its flute—clear, ethereal, almost
eerie notes. The dog, dozing on the grass,
pricks up one ear. I move my chair
with the sun, but he stays in a hemlock's
shadow. The bird could be a hermit

thrush, its song now a kind of scolding.
Alert, the dog sits, his ears' tents lifted.
I've been selfish, bringing us here with my
books and pencils. Years ago I stood on this
cabin's porch, dreaming I heard a bird
singing in the cage my bones make.

Whatever it was, I let it go. There is a path
through these woods—the dog and I might
yet find that thrush, its round notes followed
by a *pip-pip-pip*. But the great poets have
already given us the thrush, and the trees
are stuffing daylight into their big, black coats.

Cormorant

Luminous as an oil slick
in the sun, this morning's
cormorant rides out low
tide on a gray-green rock
you couldn't see an hour

ago. When the bird first surged
from the sea you thought
Snake. Something tunneling
down its length like a vole.
Not vole, crab. Then

the shoulders—massive,
mythic: Snake on Raven's
Back. Better, Milton's Satan
in a tree. Tempting you,
its gleaming wings spread

like great leaves to dry. There
was a time you would have
given in. You would have
said *Yes.* Swallowed
anything. Later you would

have woken cold, tangled
amidst the seaweed and slime.
That's where he found you,
your beloved. One morning
like this, walking the wrack line.

Bluebird

I carved hollows into bodies of trees,
nailed boxes on poles in sun-dazed
fields; I appealed to the oldest witch,
keeper of charms, to visit me in my

dreams, whisper where the bluebird
resides. My dead mother—the first—
appeared instead. I pretended
to sleep. She was happy I'd found her

other daughter, her son, but there was
no bluebird on her tongue or among
the folds of her dress. Soon she
disappeared, as is her habit, into

the ether. *If you ever catch that bird,*
said my newly discovered brother,
it'll change color in its cage. To him,
survival is happiness, as good as it

gets. Years later, my other dead mother
found me standing behind the house
in LaGrange, where the bird used to nest.
My mother took my hand and there it was

in my palm, a gleaming sapphire, warm
to the touch and throbbing with what felt
like desire. This mother couldn't stay, but
will come back as she can. And the bird?

I've learned its song as well as I know
my Sweet Love's face. There it is now,
tossing its notes out of the soggy field
like so many blue stones.

Sandpipers

Each morning we walk the beach, east
a salmon-pink glow. Just a few weeks ago
sandpipers threw themselves in the air
when we approached—gulls never cared,

stood their ground, haggling over a smashed
clam or crust of bread we tossed—oh,
how they shriek. This early the tide is
always out. We lean into a salt-steeped breeze

all the way to the breakwall and back. Sandpipers
wait for a wave to retreat, then fast-forward
on knobby-kneed legs, beaks needling the beach
like sewing machines. They make us laugh. At last

they've grown used to our daily going by, the way
city squirrels do, or pigeons in the parks. I've left
the city, a broken marriage or two behind. Your
wounds are sleepless, the kind that see in the dark.

We each swallowed an ocean, but couldn't hold it
in. Every day we begin again. Now we treat
sandpipers as if they're our friends—the godwit,
dowitcher, willet, the dun-colored dunlin.

Pheasant

This pheasant won't be shot
by fat men after breakfast.
This pheasant's etched in stone.
But there I go again, dreaming
of home, my father's love

of pheasants—my father long
gone. The stone is granite
and marks my father's grave.
All morning the crows
have behaved badly while

the pheasant, wings stretched
wide, waits
for a flight that never begins.
He's been ready just twenty
years, yet his rock is showing

wear. So much for immortality.
Who will save you now?
mock the crows, pulling plastic
tulips from the ground. Not
the pheasant, bound by stone

into silence. Not his brother crow,
that clown, who has staked a claim
to the fresh earth mound where
my mother lies, so newly arrived
she's still saying her hellos.

Ravens

White Mountains, New Hampshire

The black dog is aged now. His breaths heave
like a rusty bellows. He no longer ventures
far from the cabin—the woman has just
helped him down the two wood steps, holding
his back-end up with a sling. All week

the road to town has been closed. From
the little knoll where the cabin sits she can see
where the road forks, the sign men in orange
vests were pounding into the shoulder there
as she and the dog arrived at July's end. Ravens

are nesting nearby again. Ravens mate for life—
considered (strangely enough, she thinks) a mark
of intelligence. She hopes by now they know her
and the dog. Hopes they'll swoop then settle
on the huge rock—as big as a compact car—where

she has placed some crackers, a few red grapes.
There goes another tourist in an S.U.V. thinking
he's going south toward town, Road Closed sign
be damned. Already the dog is asleep on the grass.
He won't be climbing Cannon or Indian Head, or

the Coppermine Trail to Bridal Veil Falls. One raven
flaps upwind overhead, carrying a furred, dark
thing. She hurries to the porch for her binoculars.
Damn. They must be here, she frets, behind all
these books. Under these papers, her scribbled

poems ruffling in the breeze. The one about
the Bee House flutters to the floor like a leaf.
And here comes the tourist again, white Ford
heading back up the hill. That's number thirty-
six today. Not that she's counting. Under the dog's

towel? Binoculars! Like the car, the raven—
a speck now over distant oaks—has also headed
east, toward Bethlehem. Surely that means
something, she thinks. Didn't ravens have some
connection to Christ? Maybe that was magpies.

Pelicans? It certainly isn't ominous, not in a bad
way. Rarely have they been that, even from
the earliest days of her raven dreams, back when
they spoke to her. Pulled at her hair. Awake,
the dog sniffs the air, eyes closed to the overcast

sky. There goes number thirty-seven, red canoe
tied to the roof rack. See you back in five-and-a-half
minutes, she says. The dog yawns. If she wears
binoculars around her neck, neither raven will show.
Thirty-eight, blue pick-up. No lie. Sign couldn't be

more clear: ROAD CLOSED ½ MILE. A handful
have turned around but most keep going, barely
tapping their brakes. What does that say about
human nature, she asks the dog. Maybe the big boulder
with the crackers and grapes is too close to the cabin.

Crows seem to her more bold than ravens. As if
either is going to be her friend. She slips the harness
over the dog's head, straps him to the two-wheeled
cart: he is his own noble chariot. Fine fog seems to be
filling the trees as a wood thrush trills her flute. See,

one Vermonter in a green Subaru turned around.
What a silly obsession, fueled by countless hours
on the porch. She's been trying to write about
loneliness without using the words rain, radio, or
moon. Scratch also mother, dog. But there—now—

there, not one but two ravens gliding toward
the Notch. She wants them to mean something.
They fly south, directly over thirty-seven and thirty-
eight, the blue truck behind the car with the canoe,
following at last the detour signs. She can just

make out Cannon—really it's all of the Notch that's
visible, its peak snagged by cloud. Blue mist hugs
its sides. Then it happens so fast: a cloud curtain
pulls itself down, down, and all is gray. Ravens
ride the foreground like a signature. The dog sniffs

the cookie in her hand, turns his head. Oh, she says.
Good boy, Mama's best boy. Later she'll take
the bucket, hike to the spring without him. For now,
he heads south, as the ravens do, down the mist-
filled lawn into cloud.

Sparrow

The House Sparrow takes frequent dust baths. It throws soil and dust over its body feathers, just as if it were bathing with water.
—Cornell Lab of Ornithology

Saint Bede said the soul is a sparrow.
It flits in one door, flutters down

a hall, disappears out another door—
a brownish-black, soon forgotten

flash. Sparrow. The word itself, from
the Anglo-Saxon, means "a flutterer."

To flutter is to float—*sparrow on
waves, sparrow on a pond.* Or flutter

is to contract, to beat irregularly—
sparrow in my heart. Or to tremble

with excitement—*I could barely
contain my sparrow.* If water flutters,

there's more than a ripple. This morning
a sparrow splashes in the garden

dirt like a baby in the tub. A soul,
perhaps, celebrating its former

body returned, as promised, to dust.
Oh, my very being wants to believe—

but my faith, that sparrow, flutters. So
when my grave's been dug, when they

lower my dust into the ground, may
a host of sparrows bathe with me.

May we fling that fresh earth skyward,
then lift our faces as it rains back down.

Sources & Notes

Ackerman, Jennifer. *The Genius of Birds*. Penguin, 2016.

Cornell Lab of Ornithology website: <https://www.birds.cornell.edu>

Peterson, Roger Tory. *Field Guide to Birds of Eastern and Central North America*, Sixth Edition. Houghton Mifflin Harcourt, 2010.

Wells, Diana. *100 Birds and How They Got Their Names*. Algonquin Books of Chapel Hill, 2002.

Wild Birds Unlimited site: <https://www.wbu.com>

References to and quotes from Diana Wells's book in the following notes are meant to give her credit and make clear where some of my inspiration came from. I have italicized words/phrases that especially echo her work.

"Albatross," p. 42: The poem referred to is Coleridge's "Rime of the Ancient Mariner."

"Barn Swallow," p. 63 (Wells, 239): "In a touching thirteenth-century legend, the Christ child plays in the mud, forming little birds, which come to life—and are swallows."

"Bittern," p. 38 (Wells, 11): "Bitterns have learned an extraordinary protective strategy. They can 'freeze' with their bills pointing directly upward and their striped bodies exactly matching the reeds surrounding them. Sometimes *if there is a breeze they even sway a little to imitate their reedy camouflage.*"

"Bluebird," p. 84 (Wells, 15): Wells makes reference to a play in which two children, "searching for the 'Blue Bird of Happiness,' are warned, 'It seems likely ... *that he changes colour when he is caged.*'"

"Cardinal," p. 33 (Wells, 25): "[In 17th century America] It was frequently captured and put in cages, where both males and females would sing 'exceedingly sweet,' unless 'they would die with grief.'"

"Cormorant," p. 83 (Wells, 34): "Satan, in John Milton's *Paradise Lost*, 'sat like a cormorant' on the Tree of Life, watching Adam and Eve and 'devising death.'... Their common name means raven of the sea."

"Cowbird," p. 56 (Wells, 37-38): "Cowbirds are obligate parasites, which are unable to build their own nests and raise their own young ... *Molobrus* is Greek for parasite."

"Crow," p. 20 (Wells, 43-45): "The scarecrow ... is familiar to the smallest children, although they *probably don't associate him with the bird at all*. Adults using *crowbars* don't think of the crow's strong curved bill, which, like the tool it names, is designed to pry loose and turn heavy objects ... and sailors scanned the horizon from *a crow's nest*, too." "In the ghoulish seventeenth-century Scottish ballad 'Twa' Corbies,' two hooded crows gleefully discuss dining on the body of a knight and pecking out his 'bonny blue e'en,' a common habit of corvids." (Note: I remembered reading that poem as an undergrad.) "Crows are most often associated with corpses and dark death." "Their voices, far from being heavenly, are harsh and unmusical, even though corvids are ... 'song' birds. 'Crow' comes from the Anglo-Saxon *crawe*, an imitation of their cry, although nowadays roosters 'crow' and crows 'caw,' without an r." "They were so common that before the advent of clocks, if the sky were overcast and the sunset was obscured, Hebrews would begin their Sabbath when crows came to roost at sunset." While I believe I made up the term "knowledge of crows," Wells speaks about "raven's knowledge" as having "an acquaintance with the supernatural" (205).

Regarding the poem's question, "Didn't ravens have some / connection to Christ?": there are no references to this that I know of; however, magpies "were said to be the only creatures that would not go into the ark" (Wells, 141), and the pelican has served as "a symbol of Christ's resurrection" (Wells, 177).

The line "Ornithologists claim crows have an innate sense / of fairness" comes from *The Genius of Birds*: "Crows and ravens will balk at doing work for less reward than a peer is getting" (Ackerman, 105-6). Ackerman also discusses crows' (and ravens') use of tools and their ability to recognize human faces.

"Flicker," p. 39 (Wells, 72): "The wings of flickers catch the eye like flickering light as they fly."

"Geese," p. 53: Ralph Waldo Emerson's quote is taken from *Self-Reliance*. "Everybody's Got the Blues" is a song written by Michael Jacobs.

"Goldfinch," p. 28 (Wells, 85): "The red patches on the [European Goldfinch's] cheeks and face were said to be smears of Christ's blood, left when a goldfinch tried to remove the crown of thorns at the crucifixion."

"Grackle," p. 40 (Wells, 94): "When seen from a distance grackles appear plain black, but close up their color changes as the light reflects off them, through brilliant shimmering *blues*, greens, *purple*, and *bronze*."

"Heron," p. 37: Although I realize herons are not sexually dimorphic, for the purpose of the poem I chose to call the heron "she."

"House Finch," p. 31 (Wild Birds Unlimited website): "In 1940, [House Finches] were illegally captured in California and imported to New York by pet dealers. Fearing prosecution, the dealers released their 'Hollywood Finches' on Long Island."

According to Wikipedia, in 1944 Victor J. Bergeron said he invented the Mai Tai at his California restaurant, Trader Vic's. So I've stretched the truth by saying they had arrived on Long Island by 1940.

"Ibis," p. 18 (Wells, 114-115): "Thoth, the Egyptian god of *wisdom and learning*, had *the body of a man and the head of an ibis* . . . The sixteenth century Swiss naturalist Konrad Gesner named the waldrapp ibis . . . from the German *Wald*, "wood," and *Rapp*, "raven," because of its *raven-like croak*."

"Kingfisher," p. 60 (Wells, 24): "the American belted kingfisher is *Megaceryle alcyon* . . . [which refers] to the Greek goddess Alcyone (or Halcyone) . . . Kingfishers were once called halcyons, especially in poetic literature. Alcyone was the daughter of Aeolus, the god of the wind, and the widow of Ceyx, who drowned at sea. Alycone threw herself into the sea, on top of her husband's floating body. But as she kissed him and 'thrust her growing beak between his lips,' wrote Ovid, they both turned into kingfishers. [One ancient belief is that Aeolus] calmed the sea for seven days before and after the winter solstice, while the kingfishers raised their young."

"Limpkin," p. 61 (Wells, 136): "The limpkin's cry has a quality of unutterable sadness, as though the bird is wailing in despair at the desolation of its watery surroundings."

"Magpie," p. 58 (Wells, 141): "from the time of Noah's ark, magpies have had a reputation for chattering. Magpies were said to be the only creatures that would not go into the ark, *preferring to perch on the roof chattering while the world around it drowned.*"

"Nuthatch," p. 62 (Wells, 154): "The common name, nuthatch ... comes from the Anglo-Saxon *hnuta*, 'a nut,' and the Old English, *hakken* or *hacken*, meaning 'to break' or 'cleave.' ... White-breasted nuthatches have been seen ... holding crushed blister beetles in their beak and scouring the entrance to the nest hole, presumably to deter rodents."

"Oriole," p. 76 (Wells, 157): "Orioles often use man-made materials for their nests, so the ornithologist Alexander Wilson warned women to keep 'narrowly watching their thread that may chance to be out bleaching.'"

"Ostrich," p. 71 (Wells, 162): "Actually, ostriches *don't* bury their heads in sand, although they sometimes stretch them forward and rest them on the ground."

"Parrot," p. 58 (Wells, 168-170): "Prostitutes in India reputedly carried parrots. ... [Parrots were] thought to be the original companions of Adam."

"Partridge," p. 49 (Wells, 171): "When *miles of hedges* were planted to enclose British fields during the 18th century, partridges, which hide in underbrush, flourished. They became favorite game birds ... by the 19th century the French sport of shooting birds on the wing became customary."

"Penguins." p. 30 (Wells, 181): "The male emperor penguin incubates the single egg on its feet, holding it against a bare brood patch on his abdomen and eating nothing for months, huddling with the other devoted fathers throughout a winter of *frozen nights and swirling blizzards.* If, after months away, the female's return with food is delayed, the male feeds the chick 'milk' from his crop as they both wait. ... Even sailors, who once heartlessly slaughtered penguins, *cramming them into the ship's holds* by the thousands, must have been touched by the birds. John Winter, who sailed with Francis Drake to Patagonia in 1578, described penguins walking 'so upright, that *a farre off man would take them to be little children*.'"

"Petrels," p. 41 (Wells, 182): "Petrels don't walk on water . . . but they push themselves along with their feet, looking as if they are walking on the waves."

"Pheasant," p. 86 (Wells, 188): "The bird would serve to spark a new life and love for Lady Chatterley, but was itself being raised to be *shot* 'ultimately *by fat men after breakfast*.'"

"Plovers," p. 51 (Wells, 196-7): "This bird could tell a sick man . . . whether he would live or die . . . . The plover's common name comes from the Latin *pluvia*, 'rain,' but, again, we don't know why . . . . Plovers and lapwings nest in open places in scraped-out shallows."

"Ravens," p. 87 (Wells, 205-6): "Like humans, ravens are sociable and usually *mate for life*, both habits (*strangely enough*) considered characteristics of intelligent creatures."

"Sandpipers," p. 85 (Wells, 216): "Dowitchers scurry along the sand, jabbing with their bills in what is called a '*sewing machine*' motion."

"Scarlet Tanager," p. 81 (Wells, 248-9): "In 1893, [Antonín Leopold Dvořák] took his family for a holiday to Spillville, Iowa. After eight months in New York, 'I heard again the singing of birds,' he wrote." "Others have described this bird's song as like that of a robin with a sore throat." He "incorporated the song of the scarlet tanager, a bird not found in the Old World, into his American Quartet in F." "Thoreau evidently did not share Dvořák's appreciation of the tanager's song: 'With his harsh note,' he wrote firmly, 'the tanager pays for his color.'"

"Skimmer," p. 44 (Wells, 225-6): "Skimmers skim over the water surface to feed, *rarely wetting their bodies*." "They often feed in shallow estuaries at high tide . . . they are the only birds with *vertically slit pupils* (like a cat's)."

"Sparrow," p. 90 (Wells, 231-3): "The name 'sparrow' comes from the Old English spearw, meaning '*a flutterer.*'" "*The Venerable Bede compared the human soul to a little 'sparrow,' flitting down a hall: 'It enters in at one door and quickly flies out through the other.'*"

"Starlings," p. 32 (Wells, 234-5): "A group of starlings is called a 'murmuration' . . . . In winter starlings have a speckled, or '*starry*' plumage . . . . Starlings . . . are *excellent mimics. In May 1784 Mozart bought his pet starling when he heard it in a shop, whistling the Allegretto from his G major concerto.*"

"Swifts," p. 46 (Cornell Lab's "Merlin ID"): "flying cigars," "blunt heads," and "squared-off tails" are from the description found in a search in the "400 North American Birds" pages.

"Wren," p. 40 (Wells, 272-274): " 'He who shall hurt the little wren / Shall never be beloved by men.' So wrote William Blake, and wrens in Britain were protected except on St. Stephen's Day." "Wrens nest in holes, including *the pockets of coats left hanging in a tool shed.*" Wells' book is also the source of the possible Swedish and Anglo-Saxon origins of the word "wren."

It was Thomas Hardy's *Return of the Native* that first introduced me to mummer plays. According to Wikipedia, one tradition—especially in Ireland—features mummers (actors in masks, usually mimes) going from house to house on December 26, St. Stephen's Day, performing and carrying a dead wren. This tradition was inspired by a Celtic/Norse story about St. Stephen, who was said to have been betrayed by the bird while hiding from his enemies. In early times the birds were martyred by stoning the way St. Stephen was. These days, mummers might carry a live wren in a cage, or a fake or stuffed wren.

About the Author

Meg Kearney is the author of *An Unkindness of Ravens* and *Home By Now*, winner of the 2010 PEN New England LL Winship Award and a finalist for the Paterson Poetry Prize and *Foreword Magazine's* Book of the Year. An earlier version of *All Morning the Crows* was selected by Marge Piercy for the Rochelle Ratner Memorial Award from Marsh Hawk Press (cash prize without publication). Her heroic crown of sonnets, *The Ice Storm*, was published as a chapbook in 2020 by Green Linden Press.

Her poetry has been featured on *Poetry Daily*, Ted Kooser's "American Life in Poetry" column, and Garrison Keillor's "A Writer's Almanac."

Meg has also published three novels in verse for teens. Her award-winning picture book, *Trouper*, was illustrated by E.B. Lewis.

Former Associate Director of the National Book Foundation in New York, Meg is founding director of the Solstice MFA in Creative Writing Program in Chestnut Hill, Massachusetts. For more information: www.megkearney.com.

About the Artist

Craig Kosak studied at the Art Center College of Design and has enjoyed a thirty-year career as a graphic designer. In 1995 he became the first web designer at Microsoft and helped build the foundation of the Internet we use today. His work became gradually more independent, and he was inspired by road trips to the National Parks of the western U. S. His paintings have appeared in many publications and he is represented by numerous galleries. Currently he lives on Whidbey Island, exploring new aspects of his art in the studio he built himself.

About The Word Works

Since its founding in 1974, The Word Works has steadily published volumes of contemporary poetry and presented public programs. Its imprints include The Washington Prize, The Tenth Gate Prize, The Hilary Tham Capital Collection, and International Editions.

Monthly, The Word Works offers free literary programs in the Café Muse series at the Writers Center in Bethesda, MD, and each summer it holds free poetry programs in Washington, D.C.'s Rock Creek Park. Word Works programs have included "In the Shadow of the Capitol," a symposium and archival project on the African American intellectual community in segregated Washington, D.C.; the Gunston Arts Center Poetry Series; the Poet Editor panel discussions at The Writer's Center; Master Class workshops; and a writing retreat in Tuscany.

As a 501(c)3 organization, The Word Works has received awards from the National Endowment for the Arts, the National Endowment for the Humanities, the D.C. Commission on the Arts & Humanities, the Witter Bynner Foundation, Poets & Writers, The Writer's Center, Bell Atlantic, the David G. Taft Foundation, and others, including many generous private patrons.

It is a member of the Community of Literary Magazines and Presses and its books are distributed by Small Press Distribution. Visit our website to view our 150+ titles and meet our authors.

wordworksbooks.org

❧

WASHINGTON PRIZE WINNERS

Nathalie Anderson, *Following Fred Astaire*, 1998
Michael Atkinson, *One Hundred Children Waiting for a Train*, 2001
Molly Bashaw, *The Whole Field Still Moving Inside It*, 2013
Carrie Bennett, *biography of water*, 2004
Peter Blair, *Last Heat*, 1999
John Bradley, *Love-in-Idleness: The Poetry of Roberto Zingarello*, 1995, 2ND edition 2014
Christopher Bursk, *The Way Water Rubs Stone*, 1988
Richard Carr, *Ace*, 2008
Jamison Crabtree, *Rel[AM]ent*, 2014
Jessica Cuello, *Hunt*, 2016
Barbara Duffey, *Simple Machines*, 2015
B. K. Fischer, *St. Rage's Vault*, 2012
Linda Lee Harper, *Toward Desire*, 1995
Ann Rae Jonas, *A Diamond Is Hard But Not Tough*, 1997
Meg Kearney, *All Morning the Crows*, 2020
Annie Kim, *Eros, Unbroken*, 2019
Susan Lewis, *Zoom*, 2017
Frannie Lindsay, *Mayweed*, 2009
Richard Lyons, *Fleur Carnivore*, 2005
Elaine Magarrell, *Blameless Lives*, 1991
Fred Marchant, *Tipping Point*, 1993, 2ND edition 2013
Nils Michals, *Gembox*, 2018
Ron Mohring, *Survivable World*, 2003
Barbara Moore, *Farewell to the Body*, 1990
Brad Richard, *Motion Studies*, 2010
Jay Rogoff, *The Cutoff*, 1994
Prartho Sereno, *Call from Paris*, 2007, 2ND edition 2013
Enid Shomer, *Stalking the Florida Panther*, 1987
John Surowiecki, *The Hat City After Men Stopped Wearing Hats*, 2006
Miles Waggener, *Phoenix Suites*, 2002
Charlotte Warren, *Gandhi's Lap*, 2000
Mike White, *How to Make a Bird with Two Hands*, 2011
Nancy White, *Sun, Moon, Salt*, 1992, 2ND edition 2010
George Young, *Spinoza's Mouse*, 1996